THE VALLEY OF
THE COLOSSEUM

ELECTA

THE HISTORY OF THE VALLEY

On the spot of the present-day square, known to everyone as the «Piazza del Colosseo», we must imagine in ancient times a valley enclosed by the heights of the Fagutale, Oppian, Celian, Palatine and Velian hills, through which a waterway flowed in the direction of the Tiber roughly along the route now followed by via di San Gregorio.

The valley was completely transformed by Nero and the Flavian emperors, but much of its original appearance can be reconstructed from the finds of excavations carried out in various periods, including very recent ones. Indeed, it is to explorations effected just a few years ago that we owe the recovery of the ruins of the monumental fountain of the Flavian era called Meta Sudans by the ancients and the remains of the terraces and colonnades built by Nero around a small artificial lake (Nero's Pond) and in the middle of his magnificent residence, as well as vestiges of more distant periods, which had made the place justly famous for the reason that it was located at one of the vertices of the mythical «quadrangular city» founded by Romulus on the Palatine.

Right from the founding of the city (7th-6th century B.C.), the valley was inhabited, as shown by the fact that it took part in the festive ritual of the Seven Hills (in antiquity «Septimontium», designating the nuclei of the Roman community that developed around the original settlement on the Palatine and Velia) and was included in the four-ward city of the next-to-last king of Rome, Servius Tullius.

As early as the end of the sixth century, in effect, thanks to the reclamation of the waterway that flowed by the slopes of the Velia, the primeval network of roads was regularized. It centered on the road which ran from the Circus Maximus (now via di San Gregorio) to the streets linking the Palatine, Velia and Esquiline.

The intersection of these roads coincided with the future boundaries of five Augustan regions and was marked by a sacred area located near the house where Augustus was born – perhaps on the site of the primeval Curiae of Romulus – which was to be religiously preserved and restored several times by the time of Nero.

Together with the houses that crowded the valley, the constructions of Augustus and Claudius were buried beneath the ashes of the terrible fire of A.D. 64, after which the entire area was covered with Nero's luxurious and irreverent constructions (palace on the Palatine, vestibule on the Velia, residence on the Esquiline, nynphaeum on the Caelian).

The sovereign's megalomania is attested by ancient authors, who describe in great detail and with barely concealed irony the size of the imperial residence and the sumptuousness of its furnishings.

It was not until the Flavian emperors that the

1. B. Bellotto
(1720-1780),
Caprice with
the Colosseum. Parma,
Galleria Nazionale

valley was returned to the city of Rome and took on the appearance that to a great extent it still has at present, with the conspicuous signs of the stone amphitheater and those of the Meta Sudans, less conspicuous but laden with memories of the past.

«*Where the starry Colossus*
sees the constellations at close range
and lofty scaffolding rises in the middle of the road,
once gleamed the odious halls of a cruel monarch,
and in all Rome there stood a single house.
Where rises before our eyes
the august pile of the Amphitheater,
was once Nero's lake.
Where we admire the warm baths,
a speedy gift, a haughty tract of land had robbed
the poor of their dwellings.
Where the Claudian colonnade
unfolds its wide-spread shade,
was the outermost part of the palace's end.
Rome has been restored to herself,
and under your rule, Caesar,
the pleasances that belonged to a master
now belong to the people»
(Martial, *The book of spectacles*, 2).

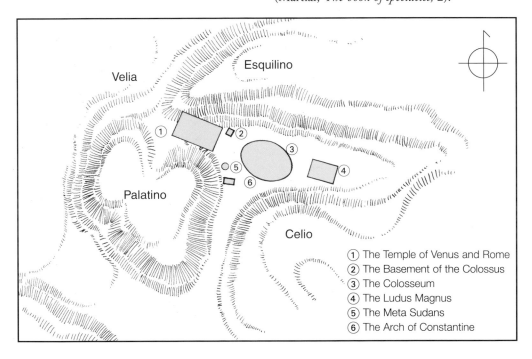

① The Temple of Venus and Rome
② The Basement of the Colossus
③ The Colosseum
④ The Ludus Magnus
⑤ The Meta Sudans
⑥ The Arch of Constantine

2. View of the valley ringed by hills

3. Flavian Amphitheater, exterior. View of the architectural orders

Works in the valley from Nero to the Flavian emperors

Nero (54-68 A.D.).
In A.D. 64 he began work on the construction of the *Domus Aurea*, which was to replace and enlarge the *Domus Transitoria* on the Palatine, extending the boundaries of his palace all the way to the Celian and Oppian hills. He transformed the Temple of the Divine Claudius and planned an artificial lake, surrounded by colonnades, in the valley. Construction work was interrupted by his death.

Vespasian (69-79 A.D.).
He planned and began the construction of the Amphitheater and a monumental fountain, the Meta Sudans, on the site where the colonnades surrounding Nero's Pond opened out.

Titus (79-81 A.D.).
He completed the buildings begun by his father and inaugurated the Amphitheater, which was connected by a colonnade to the public baths (the so-called Baths of Titus) built on the site of the *Domus Aurea*.

Domitian (81-96 A.D.).
He completed the subterranean structures of the Amphitheater and planned the construction of the gladiators' barracks (the *Ludi*) on the eastern slope of the valley.

THE COLOSSEUM

«Let barbarous Memphis speak no more of the wonder of her pyramids, nor Assyrian toil boast of Babylon; nor let the soft Ionians be extolled for Trivia's temple; let the altar of many horns say naught of Delos; nor let the Carians exalt to the skies with extravagant praises the Mausoleum poised in empty air. All labor yields to Caesar's Amphitheater. Fame shall tell of one work in lieu of all» (Martial, *The book of spectacles*, I).

The Flavian Amphitheater, commonly called the Colosseum, is certainly one of the monuments most present in the historical memory of city, and not only because of the imposing architectural mass that dominates the landscape of ancient Rome. With ups and downs, the long centuries of its history have seen it animated by a continental flow of visitors who – whether to seek refuge and lodging, perform religious rites, or work at its gradual spoliation – continued to frequent it even after the end of the gladiatorial spectacles. And precisely this long tradition kept the place alive and deeply rooted in the collective consciousness, as

well as, of course, in the cultural imagination. Construction was begun by Vespasian and finished by Titus in A.D. 80 with a solemn inauguration lasting all of one hundred days, which is recorded in ancient chronicles. As a gigantic monument to the gladiatorial spectacles that were extremely popular in the Roman world and directed to praising the generosity of the emperors who had conceived it, the Colosseum was without doubt the Flavians' most ambitious and demagogic political project.
For the first time, in effect, Rome was endowed with a facility that was equal to the fame of its spectacles. They had previously taken place in a temporary wooden building constructed under Nero in the Campus Martius after the fire in A.D. 64 had destroyed the amphitheater of Titus

Statilius Taurus, the first one recorded in the capital. Earlier, during the republican era, the games took place in the Forum Romanum or the Forum Boarium, which were provided with mobile facilities for the occasion. Under the Empire, the Colosseum was restored several times after fires and earthquakes. There is documentary evidence of work ordered by Antoninus Pius, Heliogabalus and – after a disastrous fire in A.D. 217 – Alexander Severus. Restoration work was also carried out and commemorated by epigraphs subsequent to the earthquake of A.D. 443. After A.D. 523 there is no record of spectacles. A period of decay and ruin began which in a short time transformed the monument into a quarry of building materials.

4. View of the Flavian Amphitheater from the Temple of Venus and Rome

5. Portrait head of Vespasian from Ostia, Rome, Museo Nazionale Romano

The Colossus of Nero

The name *Amphitheatrum-Colyseus* appeared for the first time in the eleventh century as a designation for the building, which had previously been called *Amphitheatrum Caesareum*, and was later extended in the name *regio Colisei* to the entire valley. It derives from the colossal bronze statue of Nero, which stood in the immediate vicinity. Commissioned from the sculptor Zenodoros and inspired by the famous Colossus of Rhodes created by Chares of Lindos at the beginning of the third century B.C., it portrayed the emperor standing and decorated

Commodus preferred to characterize it with the attributes of Hercules and his physiognomy. When the latter emperor died, the Colossus again became the image of Helios and remained such during the reign of Septimius Severus, as demonstrated by the coins of the period portraying the god with his left hand resting on a helm and his right one holding a globe. At first a symbol of immortality and later of the Eternal City, it continued to be an object of worship even in the Christian era. The base of the statue, of which only a few vestiges still exist today, was demolished in 1933, when Via dell'Impero and Via dei Trionfi were built.

«... a colossal statue of Nero, 120 feet tall, stood in the vestibule of the house. The size of the latter was such that it had three colonnades a mile long and a pool that was more like a sea, surrounded by buildings as large as cities. On the other side were villas with fields, vineyards and pastures, and woodlands full of all kinds of domestic and wild animal» (Suetonius, *Nero*, 31, 1).

the vestibule of the Domus Aurea on the site now occupied by the Temple of Venus and Rome. Its gigantic size - it was about 35 meters tall, as can be calculated from the proportions of the base and a passage from Pliny the Elder - made it the largest bronze statue ever made in the ancient world. Thus Hadrian, in order to build the Temple of Venus and Rome, had to use a cart pulled by twenty-four elephants to move the statue from its original location. Vespasian had it transformed into a radiate image of the Sun, while

6. The Meta Sudans, the Arch of Titus, the Temple of Venus and Rome, and the Colossus as reconstructed by E. Coquart (1863)

7. Model of the Flavian Amphitheater. Rome, Museo della Civiltà Romana

8. Flavian Amphitheater, view of the external ring

The exterior

The best view of the building is to be had looking at the north side (which faces Via dei Fori Imperiali), the only one which has conserved the face of the external ring in its entirety. It is divided into four levels that add up to a total height of about 49 meters and are constructed with square blocks of travertine.

The first three levels consist of eighty arcades framed by half-columns with Doric capitals at ground level, Ionic on the next one, and Corinthian on the third. Corinthian pilasters divide the fourth level into eighty compartments, of which every other one has a window. As we know from a late document and several coins from the reign of Titus, the exterior decoration of the top story must have also included shields *(clipea)* hung at regular intervals between the windows. Inside each compartment were three corbels set in line with holes in the cornice and used as supports for the wooden beams to which the *velarium* was attached. The latter was a large awning, perhaps divided into strips, which served to protect the spectators from the sun and rain and was manoeuvred for the occasion

by a special unit of sailors from the imperial fleet. The entrances were marked by progressive numbers carved above the archways (the ones on the north side are still clearly visible), which corresponded to the numbers stamped on the individual tickets. Only the main entrances, which coincided with the two axes, were not numbered, because they were reserved for the elite spectators. In the only one that has been preserved, on the north-east side, one can still see the bases of two columns of a little portico, which in ancient times was surmounted by a quadriga. The entrance on the opposite side, which was also reserved for public officials, must have been similar. Their importance and prestige were also emphasized by the figured stucco decoration on the vaults of the archways which is now hardly visible and can be reconstructed only from sixteenth-century drawings. The gladiators' entrances, instead, coincided with the long axis.

All around the monument was a delimiting area paved with travertine and marked by large stone slabs, five of which are still standing on the north side. Along the edges squared-stone construction in blocks of travertine was used for the

9. *Flavian Amphitheater, interior. Stuccowork on the north entrance in the count of Crozat's eighteenth-century engraving after a drawing by Giovanni da Udine (1487-1564)*

10. *Coin from the age of Titus portraying the Flavian Amphitheater and the Meta Sudans. Rome, Museo Nazionale Romano*

Building techniques

The Flavian Amphitheater is 52 m tall. Its long axis measures 188 m and its short one 156 m, while the total area occupied by the arena is 3,357 m². Including the standing room in the uppermost areas, its capacity must have been 73,000 spectators.
The monumentality of the building and its relatively short construction time make it a great feat of engineering. The combination of different techniques and materials (blocks of tufa were also used in the radial walls)

foundations and load-bearing walls of the area instead ran a two-order colonnade, of which a few remains are to be found beyond the modern street, on the slopes of the Oppian hill.

The interior

The present entrance is on the south side and coincides with the short axis.

The state of preservation of the stands and the visibility of the cellars of the arena, which were originally covered by a wood floor, do not contribute to providing a realistic and coherent image of the building. On the other hand, however, they perhaps help one understand the system of the corridors and interior passageways.

The different sections of the stands correspond internally to the four external tiers. The two monumental entrances on the short axis – which, as said, were

reserved for the political authorities – led to two central boxes, of which there are no remains. A series of other obligatory pathways, which were repeated symmetrically and consistently in each quadrant of the stands, led the spectators to their assigned seats.

In the first section, which consisted of large platforms with seats *(subsellia)*, was the podium reserved for the senators, which was entered directly via a short ramp from entrances located in the fourth ring corridor. Its proximity to the arena gave the illustrious guests a better view of the spectacles, but increased their risk, so the latter was eliminated by the construction of a tall and sturdy barrier along the edge of the podium.

A restoration in the 1930s reconstructed – in the usual forms of tiers of seats – part of the senators' section,

which is still clearly visible in correspondence with the east entrance.

Between the wall of the podium and the edge of the arena was a service tunnel, of which almost nothing but the back wall is left, where there were twenty-four niches faced with terra-cotta walls and floored with travertine. The complex system of water collection and channeling would seem to indicate that in antiquity they served as latrines.

In any case, the gallery was reserved for the personnel connected with the games, and could be reached from entrances located in the fourth ring corridor of the cavea and closed off to the crowd by doors, whose hinge holes can still be seen on the marble thresholds. The structures visible beyond a fence on the side of the present entrance near the service gallery (to a large extent reconstructed in the

made the contraction lighter and increased its elasticity. The vaults were in cementwork, while the walls were faced with plaster painted white and red. The floors that have been preserved are made of blocks of travertine or, more rarely, marble; on the upper stories they

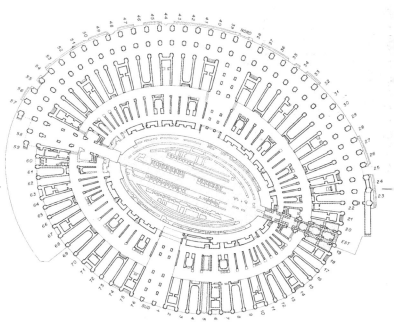

to the floor above.

The last section, which corresponds to the fourth exterior order, was made of wood *(maenianum summum in ligneis)* and crowned by a colonnade of eighty marble columns. (Presently kept on the ground floor are several capitals and pieces of columns dating in part from the restoration carried out in the age of Septimius Severus).

The complex system of ramps and passageways enabled the crowd to flow in and out with ease, but above all ensured compliance with

nineteenth century) are part of an underground passageway mentioned by sources as the site of the attempted assassination of Commodus. Still visible are parts of the black and white tesserae of flooring, marble facing, painted plaster, and stucco decoration of the vaults.

Ramps located in the third ring corridor led to the second section of the cavea, or *maenianum primum*, which consisted in eight rows made of marble. Other, considerably steeper ramps located opposite the first ones led to the third section, or *maenianum secundum*, which was subdivided into two parts, *imum* and *summum*, which was the zone

most crowded with seats. Access to these sections was also provided by stairs located in the second ring corridor, one of which has been restored and allows even present-day visitors to go up

the seating arrangements, which were strictly based on social standing.

consist of little bricks laid in herringbone fashion *(opus spicatum)*. The cavea was totally faced with marble.

on the previous page:

11. Flavian Amphitheater, plan of the ground floor

12. Flavian Amphitheater, model

13. Flavian Amphitheater, interior. Aerial view of the arena

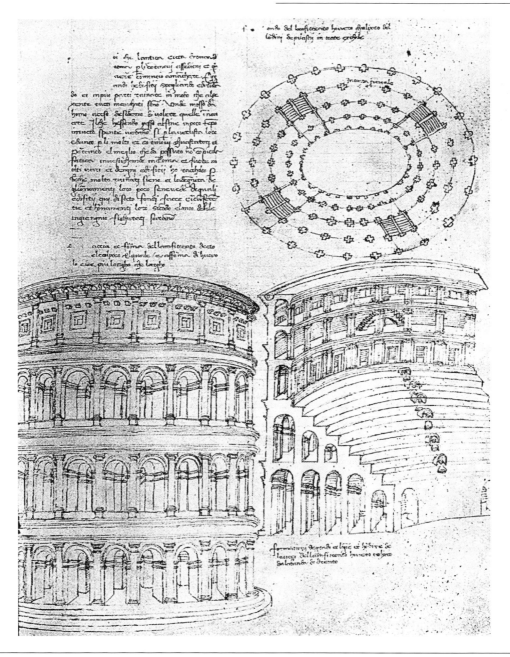

14. *Francesco di Giorgio*
Martini (1439-1502)
Colosseum.
Turin, Biblioteca Reale

Seating

Since the games were public spectacles, entrance was free. However, every citizen received a ticket on which the seat assigned to him and how to get to it were precisely indicated: the number of the entrance archway, the maenianum, the «wedge» of the latter, and the row. The stands were divided into sections according to precise social categories.
We know that Augustus carefully regulated the separation of the different classes at all public spectacles. The first section, the *podium*, was reserved for the senators, while the equites sat right above them in the front rows of the first *maenianum*. Separation was ensured by inscriptions carved on the stands indicating the magistracies, priestly classes, social categories or ethnic groups which were to sit in a given place. One of the epigraphs that have been preserved designates the place reserved for foreign ambassadors and diplomats (called *hospites*), while another one refers to the ethnic origin *Gaditanorum* (from Cadiz). Other fragments document special seats for the young *praetextati* (youth who had no yet reached the age of manhood and thus of civic duties, and who wore the *toga praetexta*) or school teachers (*paedagogi puerorum*).

An important epigraphic text of A.D. 80 designates the seats reserved for the priestly Arval Brothers, which were separated and distinguished in the different sections (from the *podium* to the wooden stands) according to the rank held in the cult. The senators, however, had the privilege of personal seats, on which their full names were written, as attested by the inscribed blocks of marble now lying around the arena, but which were originally mounted along the edge of the *podium* as a parapet. On the front is the dedication for the restoration work on the stands carried out by the prefect of Rome Flavius Paulus in the middle of the fifth century, while on the back are epigraphs with the names of the different senators carved in on the seats belonging to them in the first row.
In other cases the names were carved on the upper edge of the marble seats and as the years went by were gradually rubbed off and replaced. Those that are still legible belong to the senatorial class of the late fifth century, the last one to attend the spectacles.

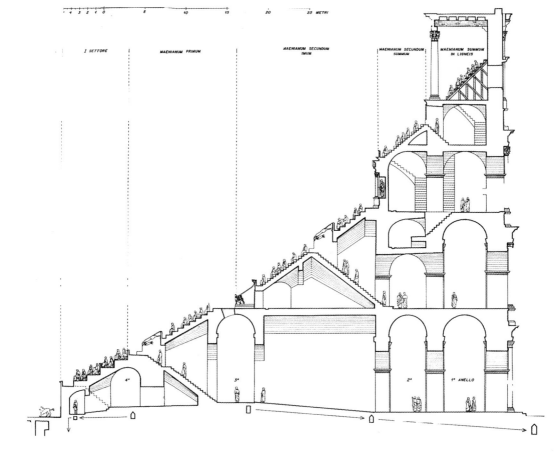

«Having been outraged by the insult to a senator who, at a crowded show in Puteoli, had not been offered a seat by anyone, [Augustus] ordered regulations to prevent the disorderly and haphazard distribution of seats. He had a senatorial decree issued providing that at every public performance the front row of seats be reserved for senators. He separated soldiers from civilians. He assigned special seats to married commoners and a special section to boys not yet come of age, as well as one to their tutors nearby. He banned badly dressed spectators from the best seats, and confined women to the highest rows, whereas they had previously sat together with men. He assigned a separate section, facing the praetor's box, to the Vestal Virgins. He did not allow any women at all to watch athletic contests. Indeed, when the crowd called for a boxing match during the Pontifical Games he postponed it until the following morning, and he issued an edict announcing that he did not want women to go to the theater before ten o'clock» (Suetonius, *August*, 44, 3-4).

15. *Flavian Amphitheater, reconstructed section showing how the cavea was divided*

16. *Flavian Amphitheater, interior. East section of the senatorial podium as reconstructed in the 1930s*

17. *Flavian Amphitheater, interior. The service gallery and the inscription regarding the restoration of the stands in the middle of the fifth century A.D. Names of senators are carved on the other side*

The arena and cellars

The arena was entered through the two gates placed in line with the long axis, called *Porta Triumphalis and Porta Libitinaria* respectively. The former was to the west and was used by the gladiators to make their entrance; the latter was to the east and was the one through which their lifeless bodies exited (in effect, Venus-Libitina was the goddes of the dead and was worshipped in a sacred wood at the Esquiline necropolis). From both of the gates steep stairways provided easy access to the cellars, where the animals and the weapons needed for the games were housed. Completed by Domitian, the underground structures were divided into four quadrants deriving from the crossing of the two corridors running along the long and short axes, where there was a series of chambers and parallel straight and curved passageways. Along the outer wall there were also service rooms, which were originally vaulted and were later split up into little cells on two floors.

The necessity of hoisting complex and heavy scenery up to the surface by systems using counterweights and inclined planes is attested by holes still visible in the corridor floor, which in ancient times were used for the installation of winches for the housing of the counterweights.

The central corridor continued underneath the east entrance and connected the cellars of the Colosseum with the *Ludus Magnus*, the nearby barracks for the gladiators. The structures visible today are what remains of the numerous restorations that took place over the years, especially after earthquakes and violent fires, which more than once destroyed the timber floor of the arena and much of the movable furnishings underground.

Until they were definitively covered by earth, which marked the end of the gladiatorial games and the beginning of the abandonment of the building.

18. Flavian Amphitheater, interior. View of the arena

19. Andriuolo, tomb 58. North slab. Detail with duel scene. Paestum, Museo Archeologico Nazionale

The gladiators

The considerable military professionalization required by the career of the gladiator had in effect created a potential army, which was organized into different teams, or *familiae*, characterized by the kind of weapons they used and the specific tactics they adopted. Epigraphic and literary sources provide us with descriptions of several categories, which are sometimes clearly recognizable in their figurative representations: the Samnite, with an oblong shield, short

The games

The spectacles that took place in the Colosseum were basically of two kinds: gladiatorial fights (called *munera* in ancient times) and mock hunts, of ferocious animals (the so-called *venationes*).

The question of their origins, especially of the *munera*, is much debated, even among ancient authors. Some of them, in effect, stress the influence of the Etruscans. They cite in this respect the figure of the attendant whose job was to drag the lifeless bodies of the gladiators from the arena and who can be compared to the Etruscan demon Charun, or recall the Etruscan origin of the term *lanista*, used by the Romans for the manager who recruited and trained the gladiators. On the other hand, other authors, such as Livy (*History of Rome*, IX, 40,17) attributed the games to the influence of Campania.

It is not by chance, in effect, that from the Oscan-Lucanian world come several funeral paintings portraying scenes of chariot races, fisticuffs and duels, which probably are the oldest figurative evidence of gladiatorial games *ante litteram*.

sword and plumed helmet; the Myrmillo, with a fish portrayed on the crest of his helmet; the Thracian, with a small round shield *(parmula)*, a helmet with a griffin's head and a curved sword; the *Rhetarius*, who was lightly armed, with a net, a trident and a piece of armour *(galerus)* on his left shoulder; the *Secutor*, with a rectangular shield and a short sword or well-sharpened dagger. The combats were usually organised between pairs of gladiators *(paria)* of different kinds, who used harmless weapons while training.

on the following pages:

20. Mosaic with gladiatorial scene, Rome, Galleria Borghese

21. Mosaic with venationes, Rome, Galleria Borghese

An efficacious expression of the ideals of strength and valour held by the nobility, the games belonged to the collective rituals of the aristocratic class of the Italic word. This explains the form they originally took in Rome: that of a private exhibition of power and family prestige. The term used to refer to them was *munera*, that is, «spectacles offered» to the community. The first ones were organized on the occasion of the funeral of Brutus Pera in 264 B.C. by the latter's sons. But their number grew so rapidly in a few years that a special law was required (the *lex Tullia de ambitu* of 61 B.C.) to curb the excesses caused by the fact that they had become easy instruments of political and electoral propaganda. The games were subsequently entrusted exclusively to the emperors and promoted only on the occasion of public events and official inaugurations.

The rule had it that they were to be called and sponsored by an *editor*, who, after settling the price of the individual gladiators with the *lanista*, saw to it that the program was publicized in good time. Accompanied by the *editor*, the gladiators entered the amphitheater just before the fight and walked around the arena to show themselves to the spectators. Among them were criminals condemned to death, slaves, and prisoners of war, but also free men for whom being a gladiator was a real profession.

During the armed duels, which lasted until one of the two was defeated, the gladiators were required to give their utmost. They were urged on and goaded by *incitatores*, the arena personnel who followed the fights close by. If one of the two did not show sufficient initiative he could be punished with death.

Gladiators unable to continue fighting and defeated ones (who otherwise would have been finished off) were allowed to ask for mercy *(missio)* from the *editor* or, more often, from the spectators. Since the financial investment involved in putting on the *munera* was substantial, there was a rather widespread tendency to spare the gladiators' lives. Indeed, the slaying of all the defeated, as portrayed in several mosaics, was a sign of unusual generosity on the part of the sponsors. Once the death of a gladiator had been verified with a red-hot iron, which thoroughly discouraged pretence, he was carried out of the Amphitheater through the *Porta Libitinaria* to the *spoliarium.*

The winners were usually given palm branches and crowns, and sometimes prize money. Convicts sentenced to death to whom freedom had been granted (i.e., were no longer obliged to be gladiators) were given a wooden bludgeon *(rudis).*

The *venationes*, on the other hand, attempted to simulate real hunts, and staged fights with or among ferocious animals. Their association with the *munera gladiatorum* goes back essentially to the imperial era, before which they were considered funerary and especially triumphal games, and as such took place in the circus. They had become fashionable in Rome following the wars of conquest in the Mediterranean, which, among other things, had marked the arrival in the city of the first exotic animals, such as lions, panthers, leopards and hippopotamuses. Promoted by Fulvio Nobo in 86 B.C. and Scipio Nasica and Publione Lentulus in 169 B.C., the first *venationes* with panthers and leopards are well known.

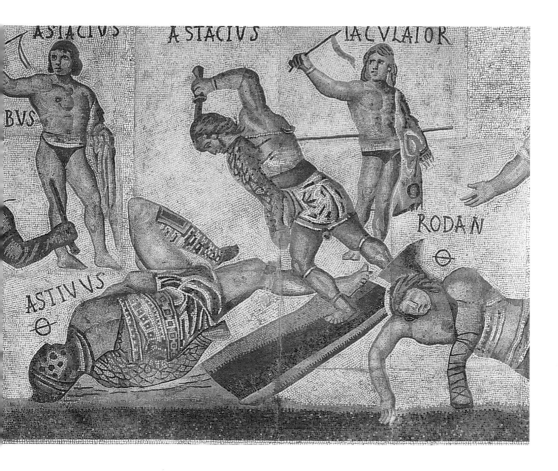

As time went by, the excitement over exotic animals grew and the triumphers began to vie with one another in exhibiting rarer and rarer ones, such as the rhinoceros brought back by Pompey in 55 B.C. and the giraffe that Caesar provided for the games in 46 B.C.

The personnel involved in these games were also convicts, and consisted of the *venatores* who led the hunts, even risking their lives, and the *bestiarii* who looked after the animals in the cellars of the amphitheater and led them up to the arena level.

Others took care of the various species of wild beasts in the *vivarii* owned by the emperor.

There were various kinds of hunts, which sometimes took place in sequence on the same morning. One kind involved the pursuit and capture of different species of ferocious animals, another a fight between two animals (for example, an elephant against a bull or a rhinoceros against a bear) until one of them was killed. A third kind involved a hunter armed with a net and was bloodless. The success of the hunts was

ensured by the amazement and excitement they aroused in the crowd. The scenery and natural backdrops that suddenly appeared in the middle of the arena, and the wild beasts and *venatores* who leaped out of them in ever new and more marvellous ways, were conceived specifically to thrill the spectators and remain etched in their memory. To celebrate the first ten years of the reign of Septimius Severus, grandiose festivities and games were organized. A *venatio* began with a make-believe shipwreck:

«... the entire cage in the amphitheater had the shape of a boat and could hold and release four hundred animals. And when it suddenly opened, bisons (a particular kind of ox, which looks strange and comes from a strange place), bears, lions, panthers, ostriches jumped out, so that seven hundred wild animals could be seen running all together and hunters in pursuit. The number of animals was seven times a hundred so that it would match the duration of the festivities, which lasted seven days»
(Dio Cassius, LXXVI 1,4).

The practice of putting deserters to death by throwing them to wild animals was begun by Scipio the Younger around the middle of the second century B.C., establishing the subsequently widespread ritual of *damnatio ad bestias*, by which criminals were punished. It sometimes took place during performances based on mythological subjects, such as the staging of the myth of Orpheus – the musician who enchanted animals by playing the flute – which, however, had a completely unexpected dénouement. According to

Martial's verses:

«The arena has shown you, O Caesar, everything which, according to the legend, Mount Rhodope admired in Orpheus's spectacle. The rocks moved slowly, and a wonderful forest similar to the garden of the Hesperides ran. Every breed of wild beast was mixed in with the livestock, and a multitude of birds hovered over the poet. The latter died, however, torn to pieces by an ungrateful bear. Only this event contradicted the legend»
(Martial, *The Book of Spectacles*, 21).

In order to ensure the continuity and regularity of the spectacles, during the republican era the aediles were obliged to provide funding for them. Subsequently the burden of the *venationes* was assumed by the emperors, who thus had an opportunity to display their generosity by conceiving more and more lavish spectacles and sometimes participating personally in them:

«(Commodus) killed a hundred bears by himself on the first day, shooting them from the podium railing. The amphitheater was divided by two intersecting walls, around which ran a gallery and which divided each other into two parts. The purpose of this was to separate the animals into four groups so that they could be shot from all directions and at short range»
(Dio Cassius, LXXII, 18).

The taste for spectacular hunts and the colorful variety of exotic animals led to a significant increase of trade in the latter. Indeed, it become necessary to establish a special imperial service. Opposed by the Christian emperors, the gladiatorial games were suspended by Honorius and permanently abolished by Valentinian in A.D. 438. All that remained were the *venationes*, which were organized for the last time in A.D. 523.

Abandonment and reuse of the Colosseum

The Amphitheater's loss of its original function led over the centuries to the transformation and decay of its structures. At first several dwellings were established in the ground-floor ring facing and everything that could be reutilized in some way, including the metal clamps that in antiquity held the blocks of stone together. In order to remove them holes still visible were made in the masonry. The plunder gradually turned several monumental buildings under construction at that time, especially St. Peter's. The Church subsequently turned the arena into a holy place: from the early sixteenth century it housed a chapel and from 1720, along its perimeter, the Stations of the

corridors. Later, in the twelfth century, the building was incorporated into the Frangipane family's fortress and remained part of it until the first half of the thirteenth century. Meanwhile, systematic plunder had already begun of the blocks of travertine, the marble sections of the monument into real quarries and even led to the demolition of the south exterior ring. A stricter conservation policy was urged in vain by Roman humanists in the fifteenth century. Indeed, excavation activity actually increased to provide materials for the Cross.

In the seventeenth and eighteenth centuries the demolitions slacked off and the first, half-hearted conservation measures were adopted. During the nineteenth century the first systematic excavations were undertaken by Carlo Fea

22. Venationes in the Amphitheater in the engraving of L. Iacopo (XVII century). Rome, Istituto Nazionale per la Grafica

23. Flavian Amphitheater, remains of the Frangipane fortress (V. Scamozzi, 1552-1616)

A visit to the Colosseum

«Rome, February 2, 1787. The Colosseum offers a remarkably beautiful sight. At night it is closed. A hermit lives in the chapel there and several beggars are squatting under the ruined vaults. The latter had lit a fire on the bare ground and a slight breeze was blowing the smoke lightly towards the arena, so that the lowest wall of the ruins was covered by it and the endless walls above took on a gloomier appearance. We stopped near the gate to look. The

(between 1812 and 1815) and Pietro Rossi (in 1874-1875). The excavations brought to light again the subterranean structures of the arena, thus making it necessary to remove the shrines and the chapel, which was originally located in the east section of the cavea. During the same period the first significant reinforcement and restoration work was carried out. Between 1805 and 1807 Raffaele Stern built the brick abutment in the east section, while in 1827 Giuseppe Valadier restored the wall of the same exterior ring on the opposite side. Finally, the work carried out by G. Salvi and L. Canina between 1831 and 1852 regarded the interior structure in the south and north sections. Further restoration, especially in the cavea and the cellars, took place in the 1930s.

moon was shining high in the sky, lighting up the smoke little by little as it escaped through the walls, cracks and openings, so that it looked like fog. This is the kind of lighting you should have when you see the Pantheon, the Capitol, the colonnade of St. Peter's, and the other main squares and streets» (J. W. Goethe, *Italian Journey*, 1786-1788).

24. H. Robert
(1733-1808).
Excavations inside the Colosseum. Madrid, Museo del Prado

25. *Flavian Amphitheater, exterior. View of the abutment of R. Stern (1774-1820)*

26. *Flavian Amphitheater, exterior. View of the abutment of G. Valadier (1762-1839)*

27. Canaletto
(1697-1768).
The Colosseum and
the Arch of Constantine.
Malibu,
Paul Getty Museum

28. Plan of the Ludus
Magnus

☐ Reconstructions

▨ Reconstruction from the map
of the age of Septimius

▮ Documented topografy

The *Ludus Magnus*

Between Via Labicana and Via di San Giovanni, the remains of the *Ludus Magnus*, the largest gladiatorial school in ancient Rome, can be seen in an enclosed area in the middle of the square. Begun in 1937 and continued between 1957 and 1961, the excavations brought to light only the north section of the building, but looking at it one can easily imagine the curved structure of the cavea. With the help of a fragment of the *Forma Urbis* – a marble map of Rome from the era of Septimius Severus, which has come down to us in fragments – on which the name of the building appears, it is possible to give a precise and complete description of the complex.

It consisted of an elliptical arena with a long axis of 62 m and a short one of 45 m surrounded by the stands of a small cavea originally faced with marble slabs. The main entrances to the arena were located on the long axis, while there were boxes for public authorities on the short one. Around the cavea there was a colonnade with two orders of travertine Tuscan columns and corner fountains (one of which has been reconstructed in the northwest corner of the area) overlooked by the gladiators' lodgings. On the north side of the excavated area, facing Via Labicana, one can see a fairly well conserved row of little cells provided with stairs leading to the upper floors. The warriors lived in the *Ludus* in a permanent state of captivity and were subjected to a severe program of daily training. A tunnel connected the arena directly to the east entrance of the Colosseum. The original construction dates back to the era of Domitian and must have caused the demolition of a residential neighbourhood of the late-republican and Augustan periods, of which there is clear evidence (the remains of a tessellated floor can be seen on the south side of the area, in the direction of the Celian hill). The remains of the cavea and the arena, on the other hand, belong to a restoration carried out under Trajan. There must have been other buildings similar to the *Ludus Magnus* overlooking the square: the *Ludus Matutinus*, where the *venatores* were trained, and the *Ludus Dacicus* and *Ludus Gallicus*, which were named after the gladiators who lived there. We must also imagine in the immediate vicinity all the auxiliary buildings we know were connected with the Colosseum, such as the *spoliarium* (where the corpses were collected after the fights in the arena), the *saniarium* (where wounded gladiators were taken), and the *armamentarium* (where weapons were stored). Probably further north, in addition, there were the *Castra Misenatium*, where the sailors in charge of the *velarium* lived, and the *Summum Choragium*, where the machinery used in staging the games was stored.

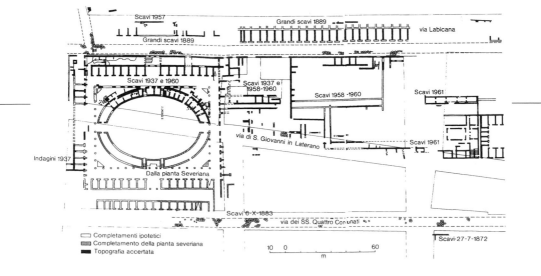

Scavi 1957
Grandi scavi 1889
via Labicana
Grandi scavi 1889
Scavi 1937 e 1960
Scavi 1937 e 1958-1960
Scavi 1958 -1960
Scavi 1961
Indagini 1937
via di S. Giovanni in Laterano
Scavi 1961
Dalla pianta Severiana
Scavi 6-X-1883
via dei SS. Quattro Coronati
Completamenti ipotetici
Completamento della pianta severiana
Topografia accertata
10 0   60
m
Scavi 27-7-1872

THE META SUDANS

In the area delimited by the Arch of Constantine, the east slopes of the Palatine and the remains of the base built by Hadrian for the Colossus, colonnades were recently brought to light that were designed and built by Nero around the artificial lake of his *Domus Aurea*. They served as a link between the vestibule of his palace on the summit of the Velia (where there is now the Temple of Venus and Rome) and the valley below. A few remains can now be seen between the Flavian Amphitheater and the circular base of the monumental fountain of the Flavian era that the ancients called *Meta Sudans*.

The *Meta* had a characteristic conic shape similar to the *meta* of a circus and was called *sudans* because of the water that spouted from it. It was located at the point where four or five Augustan regions – the II, III, IV, and X, and perhaps the I – and as many major streets converged.

The fountain consisted of a cone (17 meters tall, with a diameter of 7 meters) and a large circular tub with a diameter of 16 meters. Its original appearance can be reconstructed from coins of

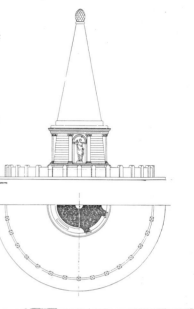

the period, which portray the niches of the base and the floral element on the tip of the cone.

What remained of the monument, which is still clearly visible in photographs from the beginning of the century, was demolished, together with the nearby base of the Colossus, when Via dei Trionfi and Via dell'Impero were built in 1933.

32. The Meta Sudans in a period photograph, before the demolitions ordered by Mussolini for reasons relating to traffic. As the Governor of Rome Boncompagni Ludovisi wrote in September 1933:«... the conservation of the two monumental remains of the base of Nero's Colossus and the Meta Sudans...is undoubtedly a very serious obstacle...obliging the cars...to turn in a tight circle...»

THE ARCH OF CONSTANTINE

Located on the Roman street along which triumphs passed, in the stretch between the Circus Maximus and the Arch of Titus, the Arch of Constantine is the largest honorary arch that has come down to us and is a precious synthesis of the ideological propaganda of Constantine's age.

The arch celebrates the triumph of the emperor Constantine over Maxentius, which took place on October 28, A.D. 312, following the victorious battle at the Milvian Bridge. As we learn from the inscription over the main arch, the monument was solemnly dedicated to the emperor by the Senate in memory of that triumph and on the occasion of the *decennalia* of the Empire, at the beginning of the tenth year of his reign on July 25, 315. The text reads, «To Emperor Caesar Flavius Constantinus Maximus Pius Felix Augustus, the Senate and the People of Rome dedicated an arch decorated with triumphal representations because, through divine inspiration and great wisdom, with his army and just arms he freed the state from the tyrant (Maxentius) and all factions».

Among the historical references of the epigraph some scholars have interpreted «divine inspiration» *(instinctu divinitatis)* as an allusion to Constantine's «conversion» to Christianity and to the legend according to which he won the battle thanks to his vision of the «holy cross». The problem is actually the subject of much debate, as is the complex question of Constantine's religious policy. In the middle of the twelfth century the monument was incorporated into the Frangipane fortress. It was restored and studied at the end of the fifteenth century and throughout the sixteenth, but the most significant activity in this respect dates from 1733, when many missing parts were replaced. The three arches are decorated by marble slabs with reliefs. It was conceived and executed during Constantine's reign as an integrated whole, utilizing mainly materials plundered from other imperial monuments. The compositional structure can therefore be divided into distinct chronological and stylistic sections, even though the choice of scenes reveals

an evident thematic unity. On the main faces and short side of the arch there are reliefs from the ages of Trajan, Hadrian and Marcus Aurelius, while the lower part presents ones from the reign of Constantine. They alternate according to symmetrical patterns and by juxtaposing different events in the history of the Empire provide a valuable sample of the figurative language of imperial propaganda: a concise overview of more than two centuries of history of official Roman art. The four panels from Trajan's time originally made up a continuous frieze and must have decorated the Forum

33. Arch of Constantine, south façade

34. Colossal head of Constantine. Rome, Musei Capitolini

35. A.L. Ducros
(18th century).
General view of the
Palatine and the Arch
of Constantine

of Trajan as part of the facing of the attic of the Basilica Ulpia. It has recently been suggested that the rondels from Hadrian's reign originally decorated the entrance arch of a sanctuary dedicated to the heroic cult of Antinoo, the young man loved by the emperor, who in effect appears in various hunting and sacrificial scenes. The reliefs of Marcus Aurelius – to which three other panels of similar size and subject are now on display in the Palazzo dei Conservatori – come from the *Arcus Panis Aurei* on the slopes of the Capitoline hill, an honorary arch celebrating the emperor's triumph over the Germanic tribes.

The faces of all the emperors portrayed in the reliefs were remodelled to resemble Constantine, with a nimbus connoting imperial majesty. The face of Licinius, the emperor of the East, appears in the rondels with sacrificial scenes.

In the panels from the reign of Marcus Aurelius, the head is Trajan's and was inserted during the eighteenth-century restoration.

The political use of images of the past

The many images crowding the sides of the arch in a complex system are actually connected and associated by a precise and evident leitmotif: the celebration of Constantine's project of restoring the Empire. He wanted to be acknowledged and celebrated as the legitimate victor over his tyrannical rival, Maxentius, and the new arbiter of Rome's future, and to this end chose a traditional monument that was deeply rooted in imperial history: the triumphal arch. He designed it to narrate his victories and crown his role in power, but decided to decorate it with older images taken from the memory of other buildings.

Diocletian had done the same thing before him, composing the so-called *Arcus Novus* on Via Lata with plundered decorations. The images of the past - the wars and triumphs of the great protagonists of the Empire - were the sign of an authority to which Constantine had to appeal to legitimize his power and guarantee the solidity of his government and his political consensus. The events taken from the victorious campaigns of Trajan and Marcus Aurelius celebrated the present (the victory over Maxentius) in the context of a solid tradition of glory and power. In the constant dialogue between past and present, the memory of the great figures of the Empire suggested a temporal continuity between Constantine and the *optimi principes* of the golden age. This consideration contributes to the understanding of the organization of the images on the two longer sides, which is based on the juxtaposition of similar themes: on the south side scenes of war and on the north one scenes of peace and public life, which ideally accompanied the triumphal procession from outside the city (South) and inside it (North).

And in this absolute and almost abstract vision of war and peace, his address to the troups (7), clemency towards the defeated (18), *pietas* towards the gods (8, 2, 4, 12, 14), and generosity towards the people (17, VI) summed up the sovereign's virtues and celebrated his moral stature in emblematic and symbolic scenes.

The idea of remaking the faces of the emperors and transforming them into portraits of himself - a well-known custom in imperial propaganda - was part of the same project. Indeed, it accomplished concretely the virtual identification of Constantine with the qualities and prestige of his predecessors.

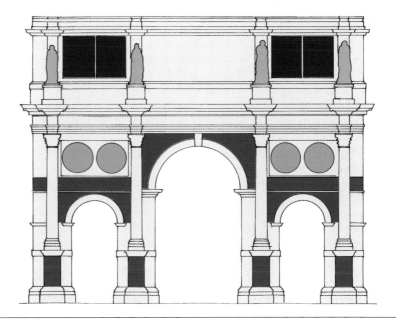

Age of Trajan

Age of Hadrian

Age of Marcus Aurelius

Age of Constantine

The reliefs of the arch

The tall bases of the columns of the two façades display carved Victories with trophies and prisoners, while on the sides of the central and smaller arches there are respectively Victories with trophies, seasonal genii and fluvial deities. The low **frieze** that runs above the smaller arches and all around the sides of the monument narrates Constantine's campaign against Maxentius, which will be read in sequence after the description. Analyzing the upper part of the arch and beginning with the **south façade**, the section immediately over the frieze of Constantine is occupied by a series of four roundels from the age of Hadrian arranged in pairs over the side arches and portraying the emperor and his train engaged in hunting and sacrificial scenes. From left to right: the departure for the hunt (1), a sacrifice to the god Silvanus (2), the bear hunt (3), and the sacrifice to Diana (4).
To the sides of the central inscription, the decoration of the attic shows two pairs of panels from the age of Marcus Aurelius framed by four statues of Dacian prisoners (A) from the age of Trajan (with hands and heads restored in the eighteenth century). The reliefs portray scenes of the emperor's military campaigns against the Germanic tribes, which were definitively defeated in A.D. 175. In order: the presentation of a barbarian chief to the Romans (5) and prisoners to the emperor (6), the sovereign's address to the troops (adlocutio) (7), and the performance of a sacrifice in the field (8).

S · FL · CONSTANTINO · MAXIMO
AVGVSTO · S · P · Q · R ·
TINCTV DIVINITATIS MENTIS
DINE CVM EXERCITV SVO
YRANNO QVAM DE OMNI EIVS
NE VNO TEMPORE IVSTIS
BLICAM VLTVS EST ARMIS
RIVMPHIS INSIGNEM DICAVIT

SIC · XX ·

Above the frieze on the **east short side** there is a roundel from the age of Constantine with Apollo/Sol emerging from the sea on a quadriga (9), while the attic displays a panel from the age of Trajan protraying the emperor in a battle scene (10).

36. Arch of Constantine, south side. Roundel from the age of Hadrian portraying the departure for a hunt

On the **north façade**, which is symmetrical to the south one, we find four roundels from the age of Hadrian portraying: a boar hunt (11), a sacrifice to Apollo (12), a lion hunt (13), and a sacrifice to Hercules (14). On the attic, the four panels from the age of Marcus Aurelius framed by four Dacian prisoners (A) depict: the arrival *(adventus)* (15) and departure *(profectio)* (16) of the emperor, the distribution of gifts to the people *(liberalitas)* (17) and a scene of clemency towards a barbarian chief *(clementia)* (18).

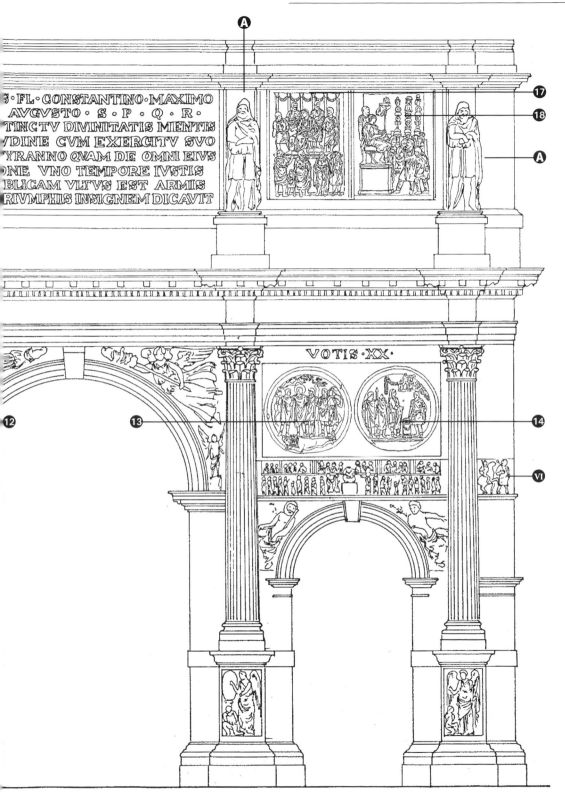

On the **west short side** there is a second roundel from the age of Constantine, symmetrical with the east one, portraying Diana/Luna on a biga (19), while the attic displays another Trajanic panel with a battle scene (20). In addition, the frieze of Constantine begins on this side with the departure of his army from the Milvian Bridge (I). It continues on the south side with the siege of Verona (II) and the battle of the Milvian Bridge (III), on the east side with Constantine's triumphal entrance into Rome (IV), and on the north side with his speech to the crowd from the *Rostra* in the Forum and the distribution of gifts to the people *(liberalitas)* (V-VI).

37. Arch of Constantine, north side. Roundel from the age of Hadrian with a hunting scene

On the **inside of the main arch**, the two Trajanic panels represent (to the east) Trajan's triumphal entrance into Rome *(adventus)* (21) with the inscription *«Fundatori quietis»* (to the founder of peace) and (to the west) a battle scene (22) with the inscription *«Liberatori Urbis»* (to the liberator of Rome).

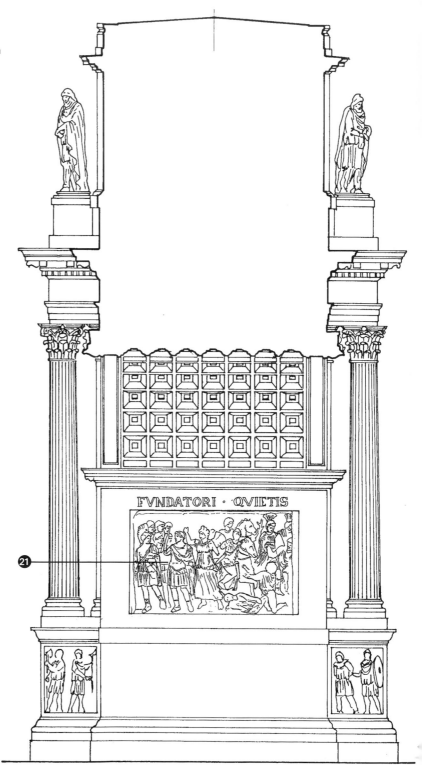

FVNDATORI · QVIETIS

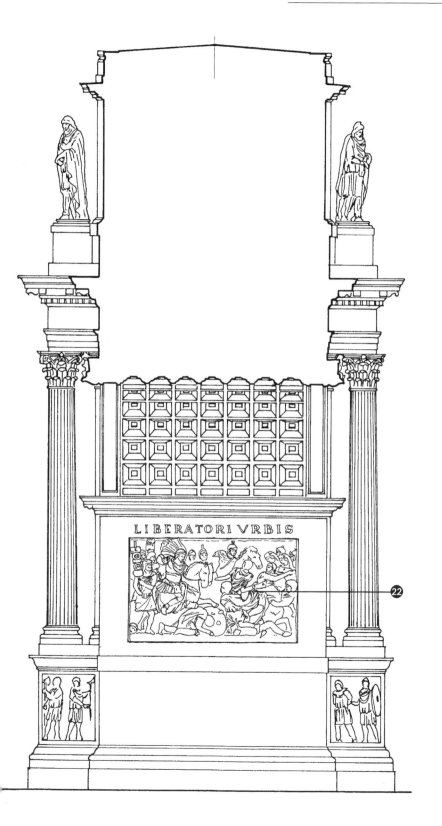

LIBERATORI VRBIS

22

THE TEMPLE OF VENUS AND ROME

The slope of the Velia overlooking the valley of the Colosseum is the site of the remains of Rome's most imposing temple, the fruit of a great architectural design conceived by the emperor Hadrian: the Temple of Venus and Rome. Begun in A.D. 121, its construction was interrupted by the sovereign's death in 138 and then started up again and completed by his successor, Antoninus Pius. The construction work led to the demolition of the vestibule of Nero's *Domus Aurea* and removal of the colossal statue that was located there:

«(Hadrian) had the Colossus moved to make room for the Temple of the goddess Rome. The great task of lifting it without knocking it down was entrusted to the architect Decrianus and required, among other things, the use of twenty-four elephants. He then had the head of Nero - to whom the statue had been dedicated - removed from the statue, consecrating it to the Sun and commissioning an identical one from the architect Apollodorus to dedicate to the Moon»
(Historia Augusta, *Hadrian*, 19, 12-13).

However, Hadrian's building respected the lines and orientation of Nero's sumptuous constructions, some of which were utilized in its foundations. The platform of the temple rested on artificial foundations and was surrounded on the long sides by double colonnades of grey granite with two propylea. The free short side left the view of the façades open. The temple was built in the middle and was surrounded by a peristyle consisting of a double row of 10 x 22 Corinthian columns. The interior had two back-to-back cellas, which housed the statues of the two divinities worshipped there: Rome in the cell facing the Forum and Venus in the one towards the Colosseum. The evident disregard in Hadrian's design of the architectural rules of the Roman temple and, on the other hand, its total compliance with Greek canons, correspond totally to the cultural profile of Hadrian, who took inspiration from Greek culture to construct his image as a ruler.

38. Portrait head of Hadrian from the Ludovisi Collection. Rome, Museo Nazionale Romano

39. The Temple of Venus and Rome and the Flavian Amphitheater

on the following pages:

40. Plan of the valley of the Colosseum

41. Temple of Venus and Rome: copy of drawing by A. Palladio. Berlin, Staatliche Museen

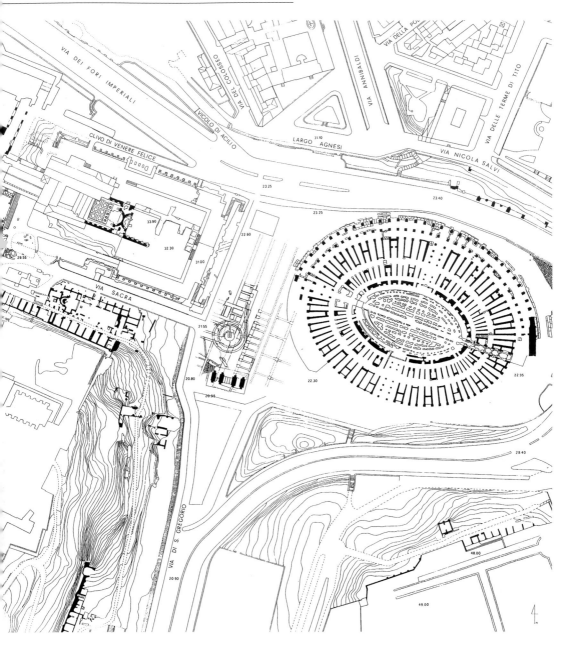

Hadrian and the cult of Venus and Rome

The dedication of the grandiose temple of the Velia took place on the 874th anniversary of the foundation of Rome (April 21, the festivity of the *Palilie*, which from then on were called *Romaia*) and crowned Hadrian's political and religious program, which was based on the cult of *Aeternitas* (of Rome and the Emperor).

The event was celebrated, among other things, by a new series of coins bearing the allegorical image of Aion, the personification of absolute and eternal time, holding a globe surmounted by a phoenix, the bird with incorruptible flesh, symbol of apotheosis and immortality. Both the new location of the Colossus of the Sun in the valley below the temple and the use of the elephants, which were also symbols of eternity, must have enhanced the evocative and symbolic power of the dedication. On the other hand, the idea of the *Aeternitas Urbis* had already been linked by Augustus to the figure of Romulus and the myth of

But it was precisely his love for Greek art that led to his fierce professional dispute with Trajan's famous architect, Apollodorus of Damascus, who criticized the temple's lack of a traditional element of traditional Roman temple architecture: a sufficiently high podium. Hadrian did not like the dispute and had him put to death.

«(Hadrian) thus sent Apollodorus the plan of the Temple of Venus and Rome to show him that even without his help a great building could be constructed, and asked him if the foundations were alright. The architect replied that, as far as the temple was concerned, he should have raised it on a platform in order to make it clearly visible from the Via Sacra, and removed earth from underneath it and placed the machinery in the hollowed out space so that all of it was out of sight and could be brought into the temple without anyone seeing it beforehand. As for the statues, Apollodorus said they were too large with respect to the size of the cella. 'If the goddesses wanted to get up and go out', he said, 'they would be unable to do so'. At this brusk reply Hadrian got extremely angry and upset, because he had make a mistake that by then was irreparable. He was unable to subdue his pride and sorrow, and had Apollodorus killed»
(Dio Cassio, LXIX, 4).

After a fire, Maxentius provided for the building's restoration, substantially modifying the original plan. It is to this restoration that we owe the apses at the back of the cellas and the barrel vaults that replaced the wood ceilings, as well as all of the interior decoration and the precious marble flooring. The best preserved part is the west cella, which is incorporated in the former convent of S. Francesca Romana, now the seat of the Antiquarium of the Forum. Completely restored in the 1930s, Maxentius's apsidal structure with its rich marble flooring, the niches in the wall framed by porphyry columns, and part of the massive vault are still visible.

Nothing at all remains of the temple's colonnades, while several columns of the ones that bordered the esplanade are now visible. All of them were restored in the thirties. A house from the late republican age was also discovered and documented during the thirties, between the podium of the temple and the Basilica of Maxentius in the northwest corner. It is characterized by a circular room in the middle with precious flooring decorated with pastes.

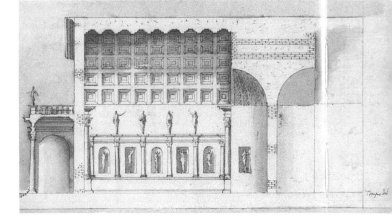

the foundation. The verses of the court poets recalled that the walls of Romulus had been built for an *aeterna urbs* and celebrated the founder as the father of the eternal city. As the new Romulus and natural heir of Augustus, Hadrian revitalized the cult of Venus – divine mother of Aeneas and thus of the descendants of Iulius – inaugurated the cult of *Roma Aeterna*, initiated a new golden age, and re-established peace in the provinces of the Empire. During his reign the image of the she-wolf suckling her twins became a recurrent decoration of public and private monuments, beginning with the pediment of the Temple of Venus and Rome, as documented by several coins from the age of Maxentius. Together with the Palladium from Troy (the image of Pallas Athena kept in the Temple of Vesta in the Forum and considered one of the talismans of Rome's greatness), the she-wolf appears on the cuirassed statues of the Emperor as a symbol of the greatness of Rome and its people.

BIBLIOGRAPHICAL REFERENCES

Colosseum
F. Colagrossi, *L'Anfiteatro Flavio nei suoi venti secoli di storia*, Florence 1913.
G. Ville, *La Gladiature en Occident des origines à la mort de Domitien*, Rome 1981.
S. Priuli, *Epigrafi dell'Anfiteatro Flavio*, in *Roma. Archeologia nel Centro*, 1. *L'area archeologica centrale*, (LSA 6, 1), Rome 1985, pp. 138 ff.
R. Rea, *L'Anfiteatro Flavio. Competizioni atletiche e spettacoli anfiteatrali: il punto di vista dell'intellettuale*, in *Lo sport nel Mondo Antico. Ludi, munera, certamina a Roma*, Rome 1987, pp. 79-85.
Spectacula. 1. Gladiateurs et amphithèatre, Actes du Colloque Toulouse-Lattes, 1987 (1990).
Anfiteatro Flavio. Immagine, testimonianze, spettacoli, Rome 1988.
R. Rea, F. Garello, L. Ottaviani, F. Severini, *Gli ipogei dell'Anfiteatro nell'analisi delle strutture murarie*, "Antiquity", 50, 1991.
R. Rea, *Anfiteatro Flavio*, Rome 1996.

Ludus Magnus
A.M. Colini, L. Cozza, *Ludus Magnus*, Rome 1962.

Meta Sudans
A.M. Colini, *Meta Sudans*, "Rendiconti della Pontificia Accademia", 13, 1937, pp.15-39
C. Panella (edited by), *Meta Sudans, I. Un'area sacra in Palatio e la valle del Colosseo prima e dopo Nerone*, Rome 1996.

Arch of Constantine
A. Giuliano, *Arco di Costantino*, Milan 1955.
S. De Maria, *Gli archi onorari di Roma e dell'Italia romana*, Rome 1987.

Temple of Venus and Rome
A. Barattolo, *Nuove ricerche sull'architettura del Tempio di Venere e Roma in età adrianea*, "Mitteilungen des Deutschen Archäologischen Instituts (Römische Abteilung)", 80, 1973, pp. 243-269.

GRAPHIC AND PHOTOGRAPHIC SOURCES

Fig. 2 and the graphic presentation of the Arch of Constantine are by Ludovico Bisi.

11, 15, 40: Archivio Grafico SAR.

28: from F. Coarelli, *Guida Archeologica di Roma*, Milan 1994⁴, pp. 196-197.

30: from A.M. Colini, *Meta Sudans*, "Rendiconti della Pontificia Accademia", 13, 1937, p. 35, fig. 17.

1: Marco Ravenna.

4: Giovanni Rinaldi, Il Dagherrotipo.

5, 7, 8, 12, 18, 19, 20, 21, 34, 41: Archivio Scala.

3, 26, 39: Archivio Mozzati.

6: from *Roma Antiqua. "Envois" degli architetti francesi (1788-1924)*, Rome 1985, p. 255.

9, 13, 16, 17, 23, 25, 31: R. Rea.

10, 32, 33, 36, 37: Archivio Vasari.

14: from S. Settis (edited by), *Memoria dell'antico nell'arte italiana*, III, *Dalla tradizione all'archeologia*, Turin 1986, fig. 86.

22: Archivio De Agostini.

24, 27, 35: Artephot.

29: Archivio Fotografico SAR.